QUANTUM THINKER

Think Bigger, Make Things Happen

Bobbi DePorter

Welcome to the
Quantum Upgrade Book Series

The world is constantly pumped full of "newness" – new ideas, facts, theories and speculation. As the world of thought expands, so must our thinking skills because there's more to understand, discover and do.

Quantum thinkers scale up their thinking skills with the five Quantum Thinking Principles. They also have more control over their thoughts and how they choose to use them, because they know their thinking style and use a powerful three-step Quantum Thinking Process to turn ideas into action.

As a quantum thinker you'll have more fun and get more done – more of the things you have to do and the things you want to do. Use your thinking upgrade to share and expand your ideas and get the results you want out of school and life.

The Quantum Upgrade Book Series:

Quantum Learner
Quantum Reader
Quantum Writer
Quantum Memorizer
Quantum Thinker
Quantum Note-Taker

QUANTUM THINKER

Think Bigger, Make Things Happen

LEARNING FORUM PUBLICATIONS

Published by Learning Forum Publications

Submit all requests for reprinting to:

Learning Forum Publications
1938 Avenida del Oro
Oceanside, CA 92056
(760) 722-0072

Cover and interior design: Stephen Schildbach
Illustrations: Jonathan Fischer
Book concept: John Pederson
Editor: Sue Baechler

Library of Congress Control Number: 2006940418

ISBN-10: 0-945525-45-1
ISBN-13: 978-0-945525-45-5

Printed in the United States of America

To the Quantum Learner who wants to learn more,
be more and do more in school and life.

Enjoy all six of our books:
Quantum Learner, Quantum Reader,
Quantum Writer, Quantum Memorizer,
Quantum Thinker and Quantum Note-Taker.

Contents

Think Bigger, Make Things Happen

Becoming a Quantum Thinker

Does your brain automatically pick apart, poke and prod every new idea and piece of information it comes across? Can you feel your mind at work as it matches, models, notices, questions, decides and judges everything in your world? Your brain was made to think like this, and you can upgrade your thinking skills in positive and important ways.

Your brain wants to see the big picture and make things happen. You control whether this will happen or not because you control what you think and how you act on it.

In chapter one, you think bigger and have more fun by stretching your mind with these five Quantum Thinking Principles:

1. **There's Always Another Way**
2. **Be Curious**
3. **Get Lots and Lots of Ideas**
4. **Find Models in the World**
5. **Stay Focused on Who You Are and What You Want**

Quantum thinkers also think differently and make important things happen with the three-step Quantum Thinking Process:

Step 1: Get Clear – what do you want to do, change or solve?
Step 2: Get Ideas – what kinds of ideas do you need?
Step 3: Get Going – what's your plan?

Chapter two shows you how to combine this process with your own personal thinking style to create possibilities and solutions for anything you want to do, create or figure out.

As a quantum thinker, you'll think bigger and get more done because you'll question, consider, examine, weigh and tweak your thoughts into actions that will take you where you want to go.

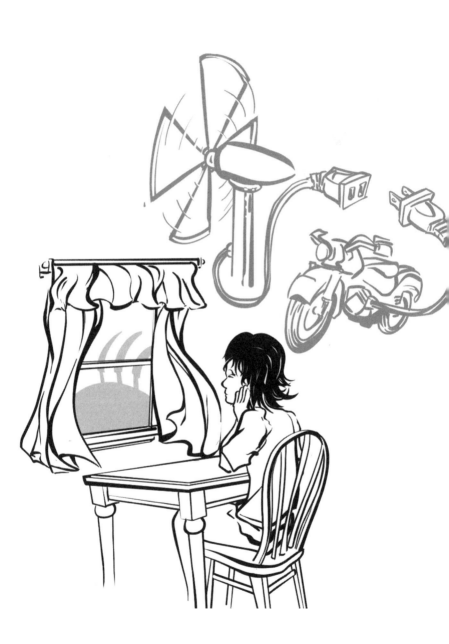

Chapter 1:
Think Bigger

Have More Fun

```
[                              ]
```

Your upgrade is in progress

What's the big idea?

What exactly does it mean to "think bigger" anyway? For one, thinking bigger creates bigger possibilities – possibilities that make a real difference in your life.

Possibility: Maybe I could link up these two computers and send messages back and forth.
Bigger Possibility: Maybe I could link up all computers in the world through a new cyber dimension (known today as the World Wide Web)!

Possibility: I could plant a tree that will absorb one ton of carbon dioxide over its lifetime.
Bigger Possibility: I could throw a party and convince all my friends to plant one tree to curb global warming by taking 20 tons of carbon dioxide out of the atmosphere!

Possibility: Maybe I could study harder and get a better grade on this test.
Bigger Possibility: Maybe I could study smarter and get better grades, period!

Thinking big also means that your thoughts match up better with this enormous world of ours. Here's what I mean:

Physically, the world is huge. It could take many lifetimes to see every part of it.

Now think of the world of thoughts – every idea, theory and interesting fact in existence. It would take you more than one thousand lifetimes to even get a glimpse of this world.

Our world is huge, especially the world of thoughts – the one only our brains can explore.

It's a big world, and you have a big brain. It's a great combo – if you know how to match them up with big thinking!

Luckily, your brain was made to scale; it was made to navigate the world of thoughts with the thinking power to match, model, notice, question, decide and judge. These are just a few of the hundreds of high-speed thinking processes you control.

You already have a big brain. Fill it up by thinking bigger and stretching your mind.

Stretch Your Mind

Don't worry, stretching your mind is not as painful as it sounds. Actually it's a lot of fun. Playing the guitar or drums, making an invention, and even some video games can stretch your mind.

Consider this: Instead of just studying about aerodynamics, you can stretch your mind by coming up with ways to apply what you're learning to ride a bike farther without getting as tired. You'll move faster and see more in less time – all because you took the time to stretch your mind!

There are many different ways to stretch your brain to fit bigger thoughts. Let's start with a right-to-left stretch.

Right vs. Left Brain:
Which Side Should You Stretch?

Now, here's an easy question: Are you right or left handed?

Here's a question that might be a little more difficult to answer: Are you right or left brained?

Like your dominant hand, most people favor one side of their brain over the other.

Left-brainers tend to be logical, sequential and highly structured. They're often good at math, science and logic games. They soak up facts and figures but have trouble with "fuzzier" knowledge like aesthetics and emotions.

Right-brainers, on the other hand, get emotions, moods and aesthetics, but cold equations and dry facts tend to bounce right past them. They're often good at art, music and drama because they tend to be more global, intuitive and sociable than left-brainers.

Which side do you favor?

You can upgrade your thinking by stretching out the weaker side of your brain.

Here's how:

If you're mostly a right-brainer, stretch your left side by doing things that involve numbers, order, logic and facts – like playing cribbage or trivial pursuit. If you're a left-brainer, adopt a hobby that forces you to use more of the right side of your brain, like painting or graphic design. Better yet, do things that force you to use both sides at once, like learning to play a musical instrument – that will really stretch things out!

Stretching your mind from right to left, or left to right, is one way to think bigger. Now make the most of this extra room with Quantum Thinking Principles.

Keep It Big:
5 Quantum Thinking Principles

Think of these principles as the five things your brain would want if it was stranded on a desert island – it's the think-big survival kit to do more and get more out of every situation.

1. There's Always Another Way
2. Be Curious
3. Get Lots and Lots of Ideas
4. Find Models in the World
5. Stay Focused on Who You Are and What You Want

Principle #1: There's Always Another Way

When something doesn't work, there's always another way to get it – if you're flexible enough to find it.

This isn't the kind of flexibility that helps you reach your toes – it's the kind that helps you reach your goals. When you're flexible, you simply find another way to make things work out.

Let's say you plan lunch with a friend at your favorite restaurant. When you find out it's closed, you try a new place down the street and it becomes your new favorite spot! Or, let's say you're training for a tennis tournament by running six days a week, but you sprain your ankle. Instead of giving up, you decide to swim in the mornings until your ankle heals. Not only do you win the tournament, you decide to go out for the swim team next year.

"When you're through changing, you're through." - Bruce Barton

Sometimes it's hard to recognize, and even harder to admit, when something's not working, especially when it's your idea. But being flexible means that you can get off what's not working, shift perspectives, and maintain the ability to change what you're doing to get what you want – it's that simple.

Think of it this way:

You're in science class and you have to come up with a way to keep an egg dropped from a third-floor window from cracking, using only materials in your classroom. You draw up a design involving a parachute made out of a trash bag and a rubber-band suspension system. Genius! Everyone is impressed with your idea and you're pumped to try it. But when the parachute breaks and the egg splatters all over the sidewalk below, you have to make a decision: find another way, or give up. Quantum thinkers know there's another way. It may just take a few broken eggs to find it!

13

Principle #2: Be Curious

Curiosity is like the seek button on your radio – it helps you tune in to the world around you.

When you were a child, you were curious about everything – and you absorbed information, facts and ideas at an incredible rate because of it. The same is true today. The more curious you are, the faster you think and the more you learn because your thinking automatically keeps up with your curiosity.

Being a quantum thinker means giving your brain permission to be curious and act like it.

But as we get older, curiosity feels riskier than it used to because we're more aware of authority and feeling "stupid." And, for some reason, these things have a stronger signal than the hundreds of questions swimming around our heads.

Today's curious minds take different kinds of field trips to feed their curiosity.

Make Magazine – **Turn your old Nintendo Game Boy into a musical instrument, build a tandem dogcart for your bike, or turn your iPod into a hard drive!**

Blogs – **Think it. Question it. Share it with the world!**

iZ – **Compose and layer wacky sounds with a toy.**

SimCity – **Find out what it's like to build and govern a city – your way.**

YOU HAVE PERMISSION TO LET YOUR BRAIN QUESTION & WONDER

"Life does not consist mainly, or even largely, of facts and happenings. It consists mainly of the storm of thoughts that is forever blowing through one's head." -Mark Twain

Principle #3: Get Lots and Lots of Ideas

Like shopping at a superstore or buying a bunch of raffle tickets, improving the selection and number of ideas in your head increases the chances you'll come across the right one.

Quantum thinkers get lots of ideas and let them "cook."

According to inventor Dr. Yoshio Nakamata, holder of twenty-three hundred patents, people who want to think bigger should stuff their brain. "Keep pumping information into it," he says. "Give your brain lots of raw material. Then give it a chance to cook."

Get more ideas in your head by resisting the urge to judge every thought and idea that comes your way.

Remember, you have permission to think whatever you want. But you don't

You don't have to say everything you think.

have to say everything that pops into your head. In fact, it's probably a good idea not to!

Another important thing to remember when stuffing your brain is that you can try ideas on for size. You don't need to believe 100% in an idea just to think it.

Principle #4: Find Models in the World

Who were your role models as a kid? Your big brother or sister? A math whiz? A popular artist or musician?

If you know of someone who's good at something you want to do or get better at, you can use that person as a model to scale up your thinking and make it happen.

Using models isn't just for kids who dream about being the next Beyoncé or Michael Jordan – it's for anyone who wants to control their thinking and stretch their mind.

People who do amazing things stretch our minds because they model what's possible.

Finding and using a model begins with a "think bigger" mindset. Most of us wouldn't think the majority of things in the Guinness Book of World Records were even possible unless someone showed us they were.

ROGER BANNISTER

A classic case of thinking bigger is the great British athlete Roger Bannister, the first person to run a mile in less than four minutes. Before he accomplished this feat, everyone thought it was impossible for a human to run a mile in four minutes. Some thought your heart would burst if you even tried! But Bannister wasn't one of them.

After thousands of athletes had trained for decades without breaking the four-minute barrier, Bannister made up his mind to do it and stunned the world with a time of three minutes and 59.4 seconds. Many said it was a fluke – that he was superhuman and that no one would ever do it again. But just one month later, his record was beaten by an Australian runner. Soon after that, many people were running the mile in under four minutes.

What was different? What snapped that suddenly erased the four-minute barrier? Was it a new training shoe with fancy air pockets or a performance-enhancing drug? No. Runners simply had a model to stretch their minds and model their thinking and training after.

People who think impossible thoughts taught us to fly. People who think things are impossible just get passed by.

When you know what's possible, you just need to figure out how to do it.

Think of something big and amazing that you'd like to do or accomplish, like compose a symphony, climb a mountain, write a book, or compete in the Olympics. Whatever your goal, you can make a quantum leap toward it by finding someone who has, or has nearly, done it already. Study their approach, thinking patterns, and motivation. Realize and believe that it's totally possible. It's not a matter of whether you can do it. It's simply a question of how you're going to make it happen. Who knows, maybe you'll become a model for others!

Following the example of a model is a way to realize what's possible. But it will only work if you can personalize it and make it fit your life.

DR. JOHN GODDARD

You may know the story of John Goddard's Life List. He was fifteen when he sat down at his kitchen table and wrote three words at the top of a yellow pad, "My Life List." Under that heading he wrote down 127 goals. These were not easy goals. They included climbing the world's major mountains, exploring the longest rivers of the world, running a mile in five minutes, and visiting every country in the world.

Now, almost seven decades later, he has accomplished 110 of these goals and lived to tell hair-raising stories and even break world records. Dr. Goddard told Quantum Learning leader Chicka Elloy recently that he had another unpublished personal list and that he has completed 600 of these 653 goals.

There is John Goddard strength in all of us. He's a big thinker who believes that age does not determine attitude. He sees every day and every moment as complete. There is no neutral. Do or do not, but savor each day. The question he would ask you today if you met is, "Who is your best friend?" John believes that you better train yourself to be your best friend. And when you review his list of goals and accomplishments, you'll appreciate the lifetime value of thinking about how to make things happen that matter to you and never wavering from your dreams and ambitions.

My Life List by John Goddard

Explore:		
1. * Nile River	2. * Amazon River	3. * Congo River
4. * Colorado River	5. Yangtze River, China	6. Niger River
7. Orinoco River, Venezuela	8. * Rio Coco, Nicaragua	

Study Primitive Cultures in:		
9. * The Congo	10. * New Guinea	11. * Brazil
12. * Borneo	13. * The Sudan	14. * Australia
15. * Kenya	16. * The Philippines	17. * Tanzania
18. * Ethiopia	19. * Nigeria	20. * Alaska

Climb:		
21. Mt. Everest	22. Mt. Aconcagua, Argentina	23. Mt. McKinley
24. * Mt. Hauscaran, Peru	25. * Mt. Kilimanjaro	26. * Mt. Ararat, Turkey
27. * Mt. Kenya	28. Mt. Cook, New Zealand	29. * Mt. Popocatepetl, Mexico
30. * The Matterhorn	31. * Mt. Rainier	32. * Mt. Fuji
33. * Mt. Vesuvius	34. * Mt. Bromo, Java	35. * Grand Tetons
36. * Mt. Baldy, California		

37. Carry out careers in medicine and exploration (studied premed, treats illnesses among primitive tribes)
38. Visit every country in the world (30 to go)
39. * Study Navaho and Hopi Indians
40. * Learn to fly a plane
41. * Ride horse in Rose Parade

* goals achieved so far

Photograph:		
42. * Iguacu Falls, Brazil	43. * Victoria Falls, Rhodesia	44. * Sutherland Falls, New Zealand
45. * Yosemite Falls	46. * Niagara Falls	
47. * Retrace travels of Marco Polo and Alexander the Great		
Explore Underwater:		
48. * Coral reefs of Florida	49. * Great Barrier Reef, Australia	50. * Red Sea
51. * Fiji Islands	52. * The Bahamas	
53. * Explore Okefenokee Swamp and the Everglades		
Visit:		
54. North and South Poles	55. * Great Wall of China	56. * Panama and Suez Canals
57. * Easter Island	58. * The Galapagos Islands	59. * Vatican City
60. * The Taj Mahal	61. * The Eiffel Tower	62. * The Blue Grotto
63. * The Tower of London	64. * The Leaning Tower of Pisa	65. * The Sacred Well of Chichen-Itza, Mexico
66. * Climb Ayers Rock in Australia	67. Follow River Jordan from Sea of Galilee to Dead Sea	
Swim in:		
68. * Lake Victoria	69. * Lake Superior	70. * Lake Tanganyika
71. * Lake Titicaca, S. America	72. * Lake Nicaragua	
Accomplish:		
73. * Become an Eagle Scout	74. * Dive in a submarine	75. * Land on and take off of an aircraft carrier
76. * Fly in a blimp, balloon and glider	77. * Ride an elephant, camel, ostrich and bronco	78. * Skin dive to 40 feet and hold breath two and a half minutes underwater

Accomplish (cont.)		
79. *Catch a ten-pound lobster and a ten-inch abalone	80. *Play flute and violin	81. *Type 50 words a minute
82. *Make a parachute jump	83. *Learn water and snow skiing	84. *Go on a church mission
85. * Follow the John Muir trail	86. * Study native medicines and bring back useful ones	87. * Bag camera trophies of elephant, lion, rhino, cheetah, cape buffalo and whale
88. * Learn to fence	89. * Learn jujitsu	90. * Teach a college course
91. * Watch a cremation ceremony in Bali	92. * Explore depths of the sea	93. Appear in a Tarzan movie
94. Own a horse, chimpanzee, cheetah, ocelot and coyote (yet to own a chimp or cheetah)	95. Become a ham radio operator	96. * Build own telescope
97. * Write a book (about his Nile trip)	98. * Publish an article in National Geographic Magazine	99. * High jump five feet
100. * Broad jump 15 feet	101. * Run mile in five minutes	102. * Weigh 175 pounds stripped (he still does)
103. * Perform 200 sit-ups and 20 pull-ups	104. * Learn French, Spanish and Arabic	105. Study dragon lizards on Komodo Island (Boat broke down within 20 miles of island)
106. * Visit birthplace of Grandfather Sorenson in Denmark	107. * Visit birthplace of Grandfather Goddard in England	108. * Ship aboard a freighter as a seaman
109. * Light a match with .22 rifle	110. * Visit a movie studio	111. * Climb Cheops' pyramid

Accomplish (cont.)		
112. Read the entire Encyclopedia Britannica (has read extensive parts in each volume)	113. * Read the Bible from cover to cover	114. * Compose music
115.* Read the works of Shakespeare, Plato, Aristotle, Dickens, Thoreau, Rousseau, Conrad, Hemingway, Twain, Burroughs, Talmage, Tolstoi, Longfellow, Keats, Poe, Bacon, Whittier and Emerson (not every work of each)	116 .* Become familiar with the compositions of Bach, Beethoven, Debussy, Ibert, Mendelssohn, Lalo, Liszt, Rimski-Korsakov, Respighi, Rachmaninoff, Paganini, Stravinsky, Toch, Tschaikovsky, Verdi	117.* Become proficient in the use of a plane, motorcycle, tractor, surfboard, rifle, pistol, canoe, microscope, football, basketball, bow and arrow, lariat and boomerang
118. * Play Clair de Lune on the piano	119. * Watch fire–walking ceremony (In Bali and Surinam)	120. * Milk a poisonous snake (bitten by diamondback during photo session)
121. * Become a member of the Explorer's Club and the Adventure's Club	122. * Learn to play polo	123. * Travel through the Grand Canyon on foot and by boat
124. * Circumnavigate the globe (four times)	125. Visit the moon ("Someday, if God wills")	126. * Marry and have children (has five children)
127. * Live to see the 21st century		

What's on your life list?

Principle #5: Stay Focused on Who You Are and What You Want

This principle is more than just a warm, fuzzy feeling: It's about finding the best way to get from point A to point B and enjoying the ride.

If you feel a rush of satisfaction after solving complicated theories or mathematical equations, feed this natural excitement and curiosity and see where it takes you.

When you're focused on what you love, you may discover new strengths and interests along the way. If you love dancing, push yourself to think of new

> Think bigger and anchor your thoughts to who you are and what you want.

ways to explore your passion. Check out different genres like tango, salsa, hip-hop and foxtrot. Learn the music, meaning and stories behind each move. In the process, you may realize that you enjoy the study of history or anthropology more than you ever realized – you just never experienced the subjects through something you really care about, like dance.

Staying focused on who you are and what you want means keeping what works for you and changing what doesn't match up. Along the way, look back to notice patterns in thinking and actions that will keep you heading in the right direction.

Did you know that you actually have the same number of brain neurons – 100 billion – as famous thinkers like da Vinci and Newton? We all do. Yet each of us has a totally unique set of interests, curiosities and passions. That's how we keep coming up with new ideas and making new discoveries. We all think differently because we are different – that's how we get more done and that's what the next chapter is all about.

The only way to get somewhere
new is to follow the real you!
You are the secret ingredient.

Chapter 2:
Think Differently

Get More Done

Your upgrade is 50% complete

You have two choices in life: You can dissolve into the mainstream, or you can be distinct. To be distinct you must be true to your unique thinking and feelings, and share them with others.

It's the differences, not the similarities, in our thinking that have taken us from the Stone Age to cyberspace.

Realizing how your thoughts are different from everyone else's helps you share them with other people to create more possibilities and solutions in your life. This is positive diversity.

We Think Differently
4 Suburban Myths about Teens

Myth 1: Teens are apathetic to learning.
Reality: Teens are non-stop learners.

Myth 2: Teens waste their minds on video games.
Reality: Teens decode and create games as well as play them.

Myth 3: Teens lose their innate curiosity.
Reality: Teen curiosity has no OFF switch.

Myth 4: Teens believe they are entitled to whatever they want.
Reality: Teens yearn to know how to take responsibility to earn their success.

Know Your Thinking Style
Express Yourself Better

Knowing your thinking style – and how it fits with other styles – helps you get more done because you can relate your ideas to others. You can bounce your ideas off other brains and get them back more developed and packed with energy than before – but first, a TV timeout.

Have you ever wondered how the producers of your favorite reality TV programs can pick a cast with

such a strong mix of opinion? It's simple: They know how to identify different thinking styles. TV producers know which thinking styles will work best together and which have stronger differences. They use this awareness to loosely control what happens on their set.

You can use this same awareness to control what happens to you, and set yourself up for better results in school and life. Knowing your thinking style will help you explain your thoughts and ideas to others. This helps others latch on to your thinking and pitch in their own ideas and upgrades to move you forward.

When I say "styles" I'm talking in generalizations. No single thinking style can possibly capture the sum total of an individual. But knowing about these general thinking styles helps you use your ideas – and the different thinking of others – to get more done.

Different Styles

It takes different thinking styles to make the world work. Knowing your thinking style gives you insight about your own behavior and the behavior of those around you.

31

People who study how we think and learn have identified four unique ways our brains prefer to process information. We call them **structured**, **logical**, **flexible** and **exploratory**. Take a moment to consider the meaning of the four styles: structured (likes order, step by step); logical (likes analyzing, common sense); flexible (likes communicating, big picture); and exploratory (likes problem-solving, creating).

What kind of quantum thinker are you?

These four ways of thinking form the four categories that roughly describe the major thinking styles on the planet. Structured thinkers and logical thinkers prefer using the left side of their brains, and flexible thinkers and exploratory thinkers prefer using the right side to process information. Thanks to our brain's plastic nature – it changes as we do – we can actually think in all four ways if we want to.

Each thinking style is a special strength we can use to understand how we learn, and see the value in other people's thinking.

LEFT BRAIN | RIGHT BRAIN

LOGICAL THINKER
FLEXIBLE THINKER
STRUCTURED THINKER
EXPLORATORY THINKER

Structured Thinkers

Structured thinkers (STs) process information in an ordered, step-by-step fashion. Their world is physical and concrete; it consists of the things they can see, touch, hear, taste and smell. They're detail-oriented perfectionists who learn by doing. STs are great with dates, facts, formulas and lists.

Exploratory Thinkers

 Like structured thinkers, exploratory thinkers (ETs) live in the concrete, physical world. But their behavior is less structured and they like to experiment. They're more creative and open to intuitive leaps, as opposed to the step-by-step ST approach. When working on a project, they sometimes get more caught up in the process than in the out-come. Sometimes they lose track of time and miss their deadlines, but they also look for new creative ways of doing things and love to explore new ideas and systems. Sound like anyone you know?

Flexible Thinkers

 Flexible thinkers (FTs) live in a world of feelings and emotions. Most people would consider an FT a "people person." They need time to reflect on and personalize new information before making decisions or forming an opinion. FTs like to see the whole picture before getting into the details, and they dislike structured environments.

Logical Thinkers

Logical thinkers live in a world of theory and thought. They like to analyze things. LTs do well at research because they can pinpoint key ideas and information, especially when it's well organized. They think logically and rationally and ask questions to figure out the *why*, as well as the *how*, behind things.

What's Your Style?

Take the Quantum Thinker quiz on the next two pages to find out how your brain thinks best and how you like to process information.

35

Quantum Thinker Quiz

Take this quiz to learn about your thinking style and how you process information.

Out of each group of words below, circle the two words that describe you best. Go with your first impulse and be honest so you can get a true picture of your style. There are no right or wrong answers.

When you're done, let's take a look at your results by marking your answers in the columns on the next page.

1.
a. imaginative
b. investigative
c. realistic
d. analytical

2.
a. organized
b. adaptable
c. rational
d. inquisitive

3.
a. debating
b. getting to the point
c. creating
d. relating to others

4.
a. empathetic
b. practical
c. academic
d. adventurous

5.
a. precise
b. big picture
c. systematic
d. inventive

6.
a. sharing
b. orderly
c. sensible
d. independent

7.
a. competitive
b. perfectionist
c. cooperative
d. common sense

8.
a. intellectual
b. sensitive
c. hard–working
d. risk–taking

9.
a. non-fiction reader
b. people person
c. problem–solver
d. planner

10.
a. memorize
b. associate
c. think through
d. originate

11.
a. changer
b. researcher
c. spontaneous
d. want directions

12.
a. communicating
b. discovering
c. cautious
d. reasoning

13.
a. challenging
b. practicing
c. caring
d. examining

14.
a. completing work
b. seeing possibilities
c. gaining ideas
d. interpreting

15.
a. doing
b. feeling
c. thinking
d. experimenting

Directions:

- In the columns below, circle the letters of the words you chose for each number.
- Add totals for columns I, II, III and IV.
- Multiply the total of each column by 4.
- The highest number indicates how you most often process information.

	Column I	Column II	Column III	Column IV
1.	C	D	A	B
2.	A	C	B	D
3.	B	A	D	C
4.	B	C	A	D
5.	A	C	B	D
6.	B	C	A	D
7.	B	D	C	A
8.	C	A	B	D
9.	D	A	B	C
10.	A	C	B	D
11.	D	B	C	A
12.	C	D	A	B
13.	B	D	C	A
14.	A	C	D	B
15.	A	C	B	D
TOTAL				

COLUMN I: _____ X 4 = _____ Structured thinker (ST)

COLUMN II: _____ X 4 = _____ Logical thinker (LT)

COLUMN III: _____ X 4 = _____ Flexible thinker (FT)

COLUMN IV: _____ X 4 = _____ Exploratory thinker (ET)

Quiz developed by John Parks Le Tellier, educational consultant and Quantum Learning instructor.

When you know your thinking style, you can take more control of your thinking.

Here's what I mean:

If you're a **structured** thinker you can team up with a **flexible** thinker to see the big picture beyond the details. Or if you're an **exploratory** thinker you can get a dose of realism for your ideas from a **logical** thinker.

"Why, sometimes I've believed as many as six impossible things before breakfast."
- The Queen in Lewis Carroll's Alice in Wonderland

Create Possibilities

Quantum thinkers are possibility thinkers. They ask: *What if? What else? Why not?* They think in positive, open-minded ways, not in absolutes. They think and talk in *maybes* and *possiblies* and *cans*, rather than *nevers* and *cannots*. They daydream and imagine themselves doing what they want to do, and then they act their way into new thinking.

Anousheh Ansari is the world's first female space tourist! She came to the United States with her parents from Iran when she was 16, and had always dreamed of going into orbit. With her savings from 20 years of work, she created the X PRIZE Foundation that helps make space travel possible for ordinary people. In 2006 she realized her dream – she spent eight days in space aboard a Russian-made Soyuz rocket with a Russian cosmonaut and an American from NASA.

Knowing your thinking style helps you think more positively and create more possibilities because it helps you think of the things you haven't thought of yet. Let me put that another way: If you know you're a flexible thinker, you're aware that you may have overlooked possibilities on the logical and structured side of the spectrum, and you can push yourself to explore these other possibilities.

Creating possibilities also means thinking seemingly impossible thoughts.

Quantum thinkers are possibility thinkers. They ask themselves:

- **What if?**
- **What else?**
- **What haven't I tried**
- **What will work better?**
- **What is the craziest thing I can think of?**

Quantum thinkers let their ideas "cook on all burners." Your mind and body have many burners that help you think things through. Quantum thinkers take advantage of these burners, including alpha state, personal experience, and physical movement.

Alpha state is a way of describing one state of your brainwave activity that you can tap into during the day. It's a state of relaxed concentration that enables you to focus intently. In alpha state you're calm and alert, absorbing material, and making connections. You are completely focused on one activity. It could be your current favorite book, a game of chess, or a sketch of something you want to better understand.

Ned Hermann is a well-known man who taught the world a lot about how the brain works and how people use that knowledge to do great things together. One thing he practiced that you might want to try – he gave himself an extra 20 minutes in bed in the morning just to think. He found that his fresh brain and the lack of worldly distractions were a great combination for getting his best thinking done.

Using your alpha state to focus your attention is one way to cook on all burners. Another way is staying alert to how personal experience can help you think differently.

Did you ever think that you couldn't do something and then you did it? If that has happened to you, then you know how that experience can suddenly shift you into thinking differently. You start rapidly asking yourself, "If I can do this, what else can I do that I thought was impossible?" Your mind flies through the many assumptions, fears and imagined impossibilities of your life, searching for new ways to think.

	45.023	1
WIN	45.019	2
	46.928	3
	47.540	4

Success happens when you lock in your thinking on one thing and give it your all.

Finding our own evidence through personal experience shuffles our thinking. It's one way we can bust out of old thoughts and get more done.

Physical movement is a natural burner of calories, but it's also great for processing thoughts. People who live in tribal communities in many parts of the world are very good at solving problems because they use physical movement to focus their attention. Drumming, dancing, jumping back and forth, and chanting are all movements that can point your mind in a certain direction and keep it cooking on an issue or idea until you think about it differently. We can adapt this idea of physical movement as another "burner" for our thoughts by using our bodies to help us incubate problems or ideas.

Create Solutions

Quantum thinkers have a three-step process for making things happen.

Our brains are all different and dynamic. But whatever kind of quantum thinker you are, you can use the Quantum Thinking Process for solving problems, making changes, and getting what you want.

Here's how it works:

Step 1: Get Clear – what do you want to do, change or solve?
Step 2: Get Ideas – what kinds of ideas do you need?
Step 3: Get Going – what's your plan?

Step 1: Get Clear – what do you want to do, change or solve?

Define the situation. Determine the outcome you want. Define limitations. What will it look like when you reach your goal or overcome the problem. Picture it in that big brain of yours.

Write everything down. Ask lots of questions – question everything, even the obvious. Dismantle the problem with vigor and curiosity and see what makes it go.

Let's say you want to buy a new computer before next school year, but you still have to come up with $500. Write down exactly how many hours you'll have to work at your job to make it happen. How many extra shifts will you have to take? Is there enough time? What if you don't even have a job? Or you're not really old enough to get a real job? What are your other options? Use Quantum Thinking Principles like: There's Always Another Way, Be Curious and Risky, and Stay Focused on Who You Are and What You Want to help you out.

Step 2: Get Ideas – what kinds of ideas do you need?

You already know the importance of getting lots of ideas. But how do you actually do this when you're dealing with a real problem or situation? Try "slinky thinking"! Slinky thinking means that you can expand and contract your thinking to move forward – like a slinky pushing and pulling its way down the stairs.

Here's how to get started:

Come up with as many solutions as possible. Don't evaluate during this step, just scoop up as many ideas as you can – even the crazy ones. What you're practicing is called divergent thinking: You're allowing your thoughts to go in many directions – wherever they happen to slink off to.

One idea leads to another. At this stage, they're all good. Dress up the pet rabbit and create an act for the school talent show? Great idea! Write it down. If you get stuck, try quantum thinker Steve Curtis's idea: Say "I wish..." before coming up with your next idea, and let fly with whatever comes up.

Once you've gathered your ideas, cover and let simmer for a few hours, or if possible, a few days and let them cook on all your burners until your ideas boil over into AHAs. At least take a moment to reflect quietly, go for a walk, clean your room, talk with a friend, or do something relaxing and repetitive before jumping back into the process.

After you've left your ideas alone for a while, turn up the heat and start stirring. Sift through your ideas and examine them. Add insight to taste. Note the ones that attract you the most and seem most likely. Pull together the ones that go together. This is called convergent thinking because your ideas are contracting inward.

Soon your mix of ideas will be reduced to a small number of workable ones, then down to just one.

Step 3: Get Going – what's your plan?

After you've cooked your ideas down to one or two good ones, it's time to turn your idea into a plan of action. Ask yourself, "Will this work?" Get feedback. Fine-tune. Make necessary changes. Any time you come up against a barrier, return to Step 2 to brainstorm a better way forward.

The Quantum Thinker Return Policy:
Return your ideas for better ones at any time!

Let's say you were too young to be hired by a company to raise the $500 you needed for the computer, so your best idea was to wash five cars a week on your block for $20 per car for five weeks to raise the money. But you found out that not enough people needed your service.

So you selected your after-school dog-walking and dog-playing service for $7 per hour. You put flyers up on all the neighborhood mailboxes with a drawing of you and a happy dog and your phone number. This idea and plan turned out to be a big hit. You ended up with more requests than you had time for and you reached your $500 goal in only four weeks. Use the three-step Quantum Thinking Process to solve problems, make changes, and get what you want.

Conclusion

Quantum thinkers are in control of their thoughts and they know the strengths and limitations of their personal thinking style. When they want to think bigger or differently, they get lots of ideas and let them "cook." Quantum thinkers know that stretched minds stay big and they are out-and-in slinky thinkers. Quantum thinkers think in positives, not absolutes, and they ask *What if? What else? Why not?* Quantum thinkers think bigger and think differently, so they get more done and have more fun.

Your upgrade is 100% complete

Congratulations!
You're a Quantum Thinker

You're ready to think bigger and have more fun by stretching both sides of your brain and using the five Quantum Thinking Principles. You know There's Always Another Way and you're ready to find it because you're Curious and Risky. You stuff your head by Getting Lots and Lots of Ideas and Find Models in the World to make the shift from *can I* to *how will I*. And you make everything work for you because you Stay Focused on Who You Are and What You Want.

Use knowledge of your thinking styles to tag-team your ideas for more possibilities and solutions. You also have the three-step Quantum Thinking Process to Get Clear, Get Ideas, and Get Going to accomplish your goals and make things happen for yourself.

About the Author

Bobbi DePorter

Bobbi DePorter is the cofounder of SuperCamp and president of Quantum Learning Network (QLN). Based in Oceanside, California, QLN is a global education leader impacting more than 2 million youth and adults from 50 states and 80 countries with programs for personal and academic excellence. Her previous books include *Quantum Success*, *Quantum Teaching, Quantum Learning* and *The Seven Biggest Teen Problems And How To Turn Them Into Strengths*, and have been printed in seven languages with worldwide distribution.

Books by Bobbi DePorter

The Quantum Upgrade Series
Quantum Learner
Quantum Reader
Quantum Writer
Quantum Memorizer
Quantum Thinker
Quantum Note-Taker

Quantum Success: 8 Key Catalysts to Shift Your Energy into Dynamic Focus
Quantum Business: Achieving Success through Quantum Learning
Quantum Teaching: Orchestrating Student Success
Quantum Learning: Unleashing the Genius in You
The 8 Keys of Excellence: Principles to Live By
The Seven Biggest Teen Problems And How To Turn Them Into Strengths

How to Contact the Quantum Learning Network

By Phone: (760) 722-0072
By Mail: Quantum Learning Network
      1938 Avenida del Oro
      Oceanside, CA 92056

Online: www.QLN.com

Receive your complimentary *"I am a Quantum Learner"* poster at www.QuantumLearner.com.

International associate offices in Taiwan, China, Hong Kong, South Korea, Malaysia, Singapore, Indonesia, Mexico, Dominican Republic and Switzerland